POWER PRESSURE COOKER XL COOKBOOK

----- ❧❦❧ -----

Step By Step Guide For Healthy, Easy And Delicious Electric Pressure Recipes

John Carter

© Copyright 2018 by John Carter
- All rights reserved.

This document is geared towards providing exact and reliable information in regards to the topic and issue covered. The publication is sold with the idea that the publisher is not required to render accounting, officially permitted, or otherwise, qualified services. If advice is necessary, legal or professional, a practiced individual in the profession should be ordered.

- From a Declaration of Principles which was accepted and approved equally by a Committee of the American Bar Association and a Committee of Publishers and Associations.

In no way is it legal to reproduce, duplicate, or transmit any part of this document in either electronic means or in printed format. Recording of this publication is strictly prohibited and any storage of this document is not allowed unless with written permission from the publisher. All rights reserved.

The information provided herein is stated to be truthful and consistent, in that any liability, in terms of inattention or otherwise, by any usage or abuse of any policies, processes, or directions contained within is the solitary and utter responsibility of the recipient reader. Under no circumstances will any legal responsibility or blame be held against the publisher for any reparation, damages, or monetary loss due to the information herein, either directly or indirectly.

Respective authors own all copyrights not held by the publisher.

The information herein is offered for informational purposes solely, and is universal as so. The presentation of the information is without contract or any type of guarantee assurance.

The trademarks that are used are without any consent, and the publication of the trademark is without permission or backing by the trademark owner. All trademarks and brands within this book are for clarifying purposes only and are the owned by the owners themselves, not affiliated with this document.

Table of Contents

INTRODUCTION 1

CHAPTER ONE ABOUT THE POWER PRESSURE COOKER XL 3

CHAPTER TWO HOW TO USE THE POWER PRESSURE COOKER XL 5

CHAPTER THREE PRESSURE COOKER MUSHROOM MARSALA SOUP 9

CHAPTER FOUR PRESSURE COOKER CRANBERRY BAKED FRENCH TOAST 13

CHAPTER FIVE TASTY CRANBERRY APPLE SAUCE 17

CHAPTER SIX JAPANESE PRESSURE COOKER BEEF CURRY 19

CHAPTER SEVEN BABY BACK RIBS 23

CHAPTER EIGHT RED BEANS AND RICE 25

CHAPTER NINE MINI RIGATONESE BOLOGNESE 27

CHAPTER TEN PRESSURE COOKER STUFFED GREEN PEPPER CASSEROLE 29

CHAPTER ELEVEN PRESSURE COOKER GREEN CHILE PORK CARNITAS 31

CHAPTER TWELVE PRESSURE COOKER CRUSTLESS TOMATO SPINACH QUICHE 35

CHAPTER THIRTEEN CHOCOLATE POT DE CREME 37

CHAPTER FOURTEEN PRESSURE COOKER SMOKY HAM HOCK AND PINTO BEAN SOUP 39

CHAPTER FIFTEEN PRESSURE COOKER KOREAN CHICKEN THIGHS 41

CHAPTER SIXTEEN PRESSURE COOKER VEGETABLE BEEF AND RICE SOUP 45

CHAPTER SEVENTEEN PRESSURE COOKER ORANGE CHICKEN 47

CHAPTER EIGHTEEN PRESSURE COOKER PULLED PORK 49

CHAPTER NINETEEN LOADED INSTANT POT MAC AND CHEESE 53

CHAPTER TWENTY NEW YORK INSTANT POT CHEESE CAKE 57

CHAPTER TWENTY ONE PRESSURE COOKER BEEF STROGANOFF 63

CHAPTER TWENTY TWO TABOULI SALAD 65

CHAPTER TWENTY THREE SWEET POTATO 67

CHAPTER TWENTY FOUR THAI PEANUT NOODLE 69

CHAPTER TWENTY FIVE PRESSURE COOKER SPAGHETTI SQUASH 71

CHAPTER TWENTY SIX PICADILLO 73

CHAPTER TWENTY SEVEN PEACH AND CHERRY COMPOTE 75

CHAPTER TWENTY EIGHT MEXICAN STREET CORN 77

CHAPTER TWENTY NINE INSTANT POT TERIYAKI CHICKEN AND RICE 79

CHAPTER THIRTY BBQ INSTANT POT RIBS 83

CHAPTER THIRTY ONE PRESSURE COOKER CHAR SIU (CHINESE BBQ PORK) 85

CHAPTER THIRTY TWO PRESSURE COOKER PORK CHOPS IN HK TOMATO SAUCE 89

CHAPTER THIRTY THREE PRESSURE COOKER CHICKEN CONGEE 93

CHAPTER THIRTY FOUR PRESSURE COOKER CREAMY ENCHILADA SOUP 95

CHAPTER FIVE PRESSURE COOKER HONEY SESAME CHICKEN 99

CHAPTER THIRTY SIX PRESSURE COOKER MEATBALLS IN EASY TOMATO SAUCE 101

CHAPTER THIRTY SEVEN POTATO LEEK SOUP 105

CHAPTER THIRTY EIGHT SOUTHERN SAUSAGE GRAVY 107

CHAPTER THIRTY NINE AVOCADO CHICKEN SOUP 109

CHAPTER FORTY SLOPPY JOES 111

CHAPTER FORTY-ONE CIOPPINO 113

CHAPTER FORTY TWO PUMPKIN SPICE RISOTTO 115

CHAPTER FORTY THREE POMEGRANATE LEG OF LAMB 117

CHAPTER FORTY FOUR LOADED MASHED POTATOES 119

CHAPTER FORTY FIVE GLAZED CARROT 121

CHAPTER FORTY SIX PRESSURE COOKER BBQ WINGS 123

CHAPTER FORTY SEVEN MOIST AND TENDER PRESSURE COOKER TURKEY BREAST 125

CHAPTER FORTY EIGHT PRESSURE COOKER PUMPKIN CRÈME BRÛLÉE 127

CHAPTER FORTY NINE PRESSURE COOKER TURKEY STOCK 131

CHAPTER FIFTY PRESSURE COOKER DATE BROWN RICE PUDDING... 133

CHAPTER FIFTY ONE PRESSURE COOKER STUFFING 135

CHAPTER FIFTY TWO PRESSURE COOKER BUTTERNUT SQUASH BUTTER 137

INTRODUCTION

The Power Pressure Cooker XL will make your cooking very easy!

Cooking has in no way been easier with the Power Pressure Cooker XL. The Power Pressure Cooker XL is very efficient — using the power pressure of steam to cook so fast and so luxuriously. With only a push of a button, you get to prepare all your favorite delicacies with all of their minerals and vitamins locked in them.

From sautéing, stewing and steaming to canning, slow cooking, warming and lots more, the Power Pressure Cooker XL, with its One-Touch Preset Buttons, Pre-Programmed Smart Settings and Flavor Infusion Technology has been designed to make cooking a fast and incredibly enjoyable experience.

In this book are delicious electric power pressure cooker recipes that include breakfast, brunch, beef, pork, poultry, pork, vegetables, seafood, stews, soups, desserts and more. Meat and seafood cooked in Your Power Pressure Cooker XL will retain their intense flavor without extra fat; vegetables also come out tender-crisp, with their fiber in one piece. For people who love to eat nutritious home-cooked meals, this book is created for you!

What then are you waiting for? Cook delicious meals in your Power Pressure Cooker XL Today!

CHAPTER ONE
ABOUT THE POWER PRESSURE COOKER XL

The Power Pressure Cooker XL is a digital pressure cooker that says it is a "one button, one pot kitchen miracle" helping you to prepare all of your most preferred slow-cooked meals in a fraction of the time.

Due to this, the Power Pressure Cooker XL claims to help you prepare succulent, wholesome meals with just one touch of a button and up to 70% faster than the conventional methods, saving you more time, energy, and money.

You can prepare your favorite slow-cooked recipes 70% faster and make one-pot meals with just a touch of a button with the Electric Power Pressure Cooker XL. It features flavor infusion technology that helps lock in flavor and nutrients for tasty and healthier results.

- Electric Power Pressure Cooker XL lets you cook delicious, flavorful and healthier meals up to 70% faster than traditional cookware and is also good for canning fruits, vegetables, and more

- Intelligent one touch preset options makes room for you to perfectly cook meat, fish, vegetables, beans, rice, soup or stews with just a press of a button

- Flavor infusion technology keeps super heated steam inside the pot to force liquid and moisture into your food, locking in strong flavor and nutrients

POWER PRESSURE COOKER XL COOKBOOK

- Push-button control panel with digital display
- Slow cooker function without stress and perfectly makes your favorite slow-cooked recipes 10x faster
- Safe lock lid with manual steam release
- Manual pressure and cooking time adjustments
- Automatic keep warm mode
- Large and sturdy lid arm handle

CHAPTER TWO
HOW TO USE THE POWER PRESSURE COOKER XL

All the pressure cooker buttons cook in the same manner except the canning button. So it doesn't matter which button you use, just chose the button with the closest cook time to the time in the recipe you want to cook.

The Power Pressure Cooker XL pressure buttons:

- Fish/Vegetables/Steam – 2 minute cook time. With the cook time selector, adjust your cook time to 4 or 10 minutes. This is the shortest cook time available on the Power Pressure Cooker XL

- Beans/Lentils – 5 minute cook time. Use the cook time selector to adjust your cook time to 15 or 30 minutes.

- Rice/Risotto – 6 minute cook time. Use the cook time selector to adjust to 18 or 25 minutes. The manual recommends using 6 minutes for white rice, 18 minutes for brown rice, and 25 minutes for wild rice.

- Soup/Stew – 10 minute cook time. Use the cook time selector to adjust the cook time to 30 or 60 minutes.

- Rice/Risotto – 6 minute cook time, use the cook time selector to adjust to 18 or 25 minutes. The manual recommends using 6 minutes for white rice, 18 minutes for brown rice, and 25 minutes for wild rice.

POWER PRESSURE COOKER XL COOKBOOK

- Soup/Stew – 10 minute cook time, use the cook time selector to adjust to 30 or 60 minutes.

- Meat/Chicken – 15 minute cook time, use the cook time selector to adjust to 40 or 60 minutes.

Additional Power Pressure Cooker XL buttons:

- Canning – the canning button cooks at 12 psi, which is high pressure in the Instant Pot. If you please, you can do all your pressure cooking with the canning button if you're pressure cooking longer than 10 minutes. You can regulate the time to 45 and 120 minutes. The Power Pressure Cooker manual does not suggest pressure canning if you are at an altitude above 2,000 ft. However, a division of the USDA warned consumers against pressure canning in digital (electric) pressure cookers. Hot water bath canning is harmless

- Slow Cook – 2 hour cook time. Use the cook time selector to adjust to 6 hours or 12 hours.

- Keep Warm/Cancel Button – Use this button to cancel a function or turn off your pressure cooker. When you pressure cooking time is up, it will automatically switch to Keep Warm.

- Delay Timer – This lets you set the pressure cooker to start cooking later in the day.

How to Sauté or brown in the Power Pressure Cooker XL

The Power Pressure Cooker doesn't come with a sauté button. Instead it recommends using the pressure cooking buttons without the lid on. Since the meat or chicken button has the longest cook time, it's a great choice for sautéing and browning. (However, it's been reported that new models now come with a sauté button!)

Releasing the Pressure

The symbols on the pressure valve are really easy to understand on the Power Pressure Cooker XL. Line up the image of the steam coming out with the triangle to hurriedly release the pressure – the open position. Line up the circle and the two triangles to pressure cook –the locked position.

The Power Pressure Cooker XL lid has an outer lid and an inner liner with a gasket. When you are cleaning the lid, make sure you remove and clean the liner – use the pull tab to separate the liner and gasket from the lid. Also remove the gasket from the liner and wash it.

When you're reattaching the liner and the gasket to the lid, make sure the pull tab is visible.

CHAPTER THREE
PRESSURE COOKER MUSHROOM MARSALA SOUP

Pressure Cooker Mushroom Marsala Soup is prepared with fresh ingredients for the finest flavor. Rosemary, thyme and a splash of dry Marsala wine improve the earthy elements of baby Portobello mushrooms. Relax and enjoy a cozy bowl tonight.

The good thing about making this soup in a pressure cooker is the fact that you're only using one pot and that makes clean up a quick one. The hand held immersion blender used to blend the cooked ingredients is also a big help. Instead of transferring hot soup to a blender or food processor, just blend in the same pot.

Each component layered into a bowl of this creamy, Pressure Cooker Mushroom Marsala Soup is meant to charm the palate. The key notes that give it a distinctive savory warmth are the dry Marsala wine and fresh rosemary.

Ingredients:

- 2 tablespoons butter
- 1 cup onion, diced
- 1 teaspoon salt
- 1 pound baby Portobello mushrooms, chopped
- 2 garlic cloves, chopped

- 1/2 cup dry Marsala wine
- 1/8 teaspoon freshly ground black pepper
- 2 teaspoons fresh rosemary, finely chopped
- 2 teaspoons fresh thyme, finely chopped
- 4 cups chicken stock
- 2 tablespoons butter
- 2 tablespoons flour
- 2 cups heavy whipping cream
- Freshly grated Parmesan and chopped parsley for garnish

How to prepare

- Preheat the pressure cooker. Melt 2 tablespoons butter. Add in the onion and one teaspoon of salt. Sauté it for two minutes.
- Add in the mushrooms, garlic and pepper. Sauté them until the mushrooms begin to discharge their moisture. Add in Marsala wine and sauté 2 minutes. Add in chicken stock, rosemary, and thyme.
- Position the lid on and turn to locked position. Turn the steam release valve to sealing. Select high pressure and 3 minutes cook time.

- While the mixture is cooking, melt 2 tablespoons butter in a sauté pan over medium-high heat. Whisk in 2 tablespoons of flour a little at a time until even. Cook for one minute, remove from heat and set aside.

- When the timer beeps, use a quick pressure release. Take off the lid, press the sauté button and allow the mixture to come to a boil. Mix in the butter and flour mixture and boil for 2 minutes. Turn off pressure cooker, and use an immersion blender to blend the mixture till smooth.

- Stir in the cream and ladle the soup into serving bowls.

- Garnish with fresh slices of Portobello mushrooms, freshly grated Parmesan and chopped parsley.

- Set a couple of the mushrooms aside and slice for garnishing the finished soup.

CHAPTER FOUR
PRESSURE COOKER CRANBERRY BAKED FRENCH TOAST

This luscious Pressure Cooker Cranberry Baked French Toast is the ideal holiday breakfast. Tart fresh cranberries in a sweet orange sauce are topped with cubed Challah bread soaked in butter, milk, and eggs, and then "baked" to make a bread pudding style French toast.

Ingredients:

Cranberry Orange Sauce

- 2 cups fresh cranberries, washed
- 1/4 cup fresh orange juice
- 1/2 cup granulated sugar
- 1/4 teaspoon ground cinnamon
- 1/4 teaspoon salt

French toast

- 4 tablespoons butter, melted
- 1/2 cup sugar
- 2 cups whole milk
- 3 eggs, beaten

- Finely grated zest from 1 orange
- 1 teaspoon vanilla extract
- 1/4 teaspoon salt
- 1 loaf Challah bread, cubed

How to prepare

- Bring cranberries, orange juice, 1/2 cup sugar, 1/4 teaspoon cinnamon, and 1/4 teaspoon salt to a boil in a saucepan over medium-high heat. Cook until the berries have popped and thickened slightly for about 5 minutes. Take out from heat. Pour into a buttered 7×3" cake pan, or similar glass or metal baking dish. (Make sure it fits in your pressure cooking pot.)

- In a big bowl, whisk together melted butter and 1/2 cup sugar. Add in milk, beaten eggs, orange zest, vanilla, and salt. Mix in cubed bread. Let rest until the bread soak up the milk, stirring infrequently.

- Spread bread mixture on top of cranberry sauce in pan. Prepare a foil sling for lifting the dish out of the pressure cooking pot by taking an 18" strip of foil and folding it lengthwise twice.

- Pour in 1 cup water into the pressure cooking pot and position the trivet in the bottom. Center the pan on the foil strip and place it into the pressure cooker.

- Lock the lid in place. Pick High Pressure and set the timer for 25 minutes. When beep sounds, turn off pressure cooker, and do a quick pressure release to release the pressure. When valve drops carefully remove lid.

- Take off dish from pressure cooking pot. If you want, place dish under the broiler to brown up the top.

CHAPTER FIVE
TASTY CRANBERRY APPLE SAUCE

This sauce is naturally sweetened, fast and easy. This Pressure Cooker Cranberry Apple Sauce will play a big role at any holiday meal.

With the combination of orange juice, apple cider, maple syrup, and a honey crisp apple, this cranberry sauce is an ideal balance of tart and sweet and is heavenly on turkey.

Ingredients:

- 12 oz fresh or frozen cranberries, rinsed
- zest and juice of 1 large orange
- 1 honey crisp apple, peeled and chopped
- ½ cup apple cider
- ½ cup pure maple syrup

How to prepare

- Pour all of the ingredients into the pressure cooker pot and stir well. Secure the lid and turn pressure release knob to a sealed position. Cook at high pressure for 5 minutes.

- When cooking is finished, use a natural release for 5 minutes and then release any remaining pressure. If liquid sprays while releasing the pressure, quickly turn the valve to the sealed position and wait for 5 more minutes.

- Simmer for 2-3 minutes to thicken. Sauce will thicken further as it cools. Serve warm or can also be made up to a week in advance and stored in the fridge. Freeze very well.

CHAPTER SIX
JAPANESE PRESSURE COOKER BEEF CURRY

This is a must try Japanese Pressure Cooker Beef Curry Recipe! Recreate one of Tokyo's most highly rated Japanese Curry Beef Stew using simple everyday ingredients. Eat this and live with no regrets.

Ingredients

- 2 pounds (937g) USDA Choice Grade Chuck Steak (Canada AAA Grade blade steak), 1.5 inch in thickness
- 6 medium garlic cloves, chopped
- ¾ cup (190ml) unsalted chicken stock
- 2 – 3 (74g – 110g) Japanese curry roux cube or homemade Japanese curry roux
- 1 tablespoon (15ml) Japanese soy sauce

Caramelized Onion Purée

- 1.5 pound (680g) yellow onions and shallots, thinly sliced
- 3 tablespoon (45g) unsalted butter
- ⅓ teaspoon (1.3g) baking soda
- Kosher salt and ground black pepper to taste

POWER PRESSURE COOKER XL COOKBOOK

How to prepare

- Heat up your pressure cooker (Instant Pot: press Sauté button) over medium heat. Ensure your pot is as hot as it can be (Instant Pot: wait until indicator says HOT).

- Melt 3 tbsp (45g) unsalted butter in pressure cooker. Add in sliced onions, shallots, ⅓ tsp (1.3g) baking soda. Sauté until moisture starts to come out of the onions (~5 minutes). Close lid and pressure cook at High Pressure for 20 minutes, then Quick Release. Open lid.

- Reduce until Caramelized (takes roughly 16 – 17 minutes) there will be lots of moisture from the onions. Reduce until most moisture has evaporated over medium high heat (Instant Pot: press cancel, Sauté button and Adjust once to Sauté More function). Stir constantly with a silicone spatula.

- Once most moisture has evaporated, adjust to medium heat (Instant Pot: press cancel and Sauté). Stir until onions are deep golden brown and all moisture has evaporated. Season with kosher salt and ground black pepper to taste. Remove caramelized onion purée and set aside.

- Brown the Chuck Steak. Adjust to medium high heat (Instant Pot: press cancel, Sauté button and Adjust once to Sauté More function. Wait until indicator says HOT).

- Lightly season chuck steak with kosher salt & black pepper. Add 1 tbsp (15ml) of olive oil in the pot. Ensure to coat oil over whole bottom of the pot.

- Add seasoned chuck roast in the pot. Brown it for 6 – 8 minutes on each side without flipping. Remove and set aside on a chopping board.

- Sauté the Garlic. Add in chopped garlic and stir until fragrant (about 30secs).

- Deglaze. Pour in roughly ½ cup (100 ml) of unsalted chicken stock and completely deglaze the pot by scrubbing all flavorful brown bits with a wooden spoon.

- Pressure Cook the Chuck Roast. Cut chuck steak into 1.5 – 2 inches stew cubes, and place them along with its meat juice back to the pot. Add remaining unsalted chicken stock, 1 tbsp (15ml) Japanese soy sauce and caramelized onion purée. Mix well. Close lid and pressure cook at High Pressure for 32 minutes + 10 minutes Natural Release. Turn off heat. Release remaining pressure. Open lid.

- Make the Japanese Curry. Taste the caramelized onion beef stew. Mix in the Japanese curry roux cubes one by one while tasting for the right balance of flavors. Taste and add more curry roux or Japanese soy sauce if necessary. We used roughly 2.5 (95g) Japanese curry roux.

- Serve over Calrose rice. Sprinkled some mozzarella cheese on top and baked it in the oven until the cheese melted and browned.

CHAPTER SEVEN
BABY BACK RIBS

Ingredients

- 2 racks baby back ribs
- 4 tbsp. granulated garlic powder
- 2 tbsp. onion powder
- 1 tbsp. cumin
- 1 tbsp. coriander
- 2 cups smoky barbecue sauce

How to prepare

- In a little bowl, thoroughly blend together the dry ingredients.
- Cut the racks into two so that they can easily fit in the Power Cooker. Season them uniformly with the seasoning blend.
- Place 1 cup of water in the Power Cooker, then add the ribs, side by side. Evenly pour the BBQ sauce over the ribs. Select cook mode then set cook time to 25 minutes.

Optional:

- Have your broiler preheated to high. Place the ribs in a single layer on a tin foil lined baking sheet and broil the ribs on each side until browned well, about 3-5 minutes per side.

- Brush the ribs with the barbecue sauce from the pot and serve.

CHAPTER EIGHT
RED BEANS AND RICE

Ingredients

- 1 lb. dried red beans
- 5 slices bacon, chopped
- 1 ham hock, smoked
- 2 cloves garlic, peeled and minced
- 2 tbsp. olive oil
- 1 large onion, peeled and diced
- 1 medium red bell pepper, seeded and diced
- ¾ cup tomato purée
- 2 tbsp. cilantro, chopped
- 4 cups chicken stock
- 3 cups rice, cooked

How to prepare:

- Put the bacon in the inner pot and set the Power Cooker on brown mode. Once the bacon is cooked add the onion and garlic and cook for 5 minutes.

- Add in the remaining ingredients, except cooked rice. Set the machine to stew mode. (Default time 30 minutes and default pressure 70).

- Serve over cooked rice.

CHAPTER NINE
MINI RIGATONESE BOLOGNESE

Ingredients

- 2 tbsp. olive oil
- 1 lb. ground beef
- 1 lb. ground pork
- 1 medium onion, peeled and finely chopped
- 2 cloves garlic, peeled and minced
- 1 medium carrot, peeled and finely chopped
- 3/4 cup dry, red wine
- 3 tbsp. tomato paste
- 2 cups crushed canned tomatoes
- 3/4 cup beef broth
- pinch cayenne pepper
- 6 tbsp. finely grated Parmigiano-Reggiano
- 1 lb. mini rigatoni pasta, cooked to preference
- salt & pepper to taste

How to prepare

- Place the oil in the inner pot and set the Power Cooker on brown mode. Place the pork and beef in the pot and cook for 10 minutes.

- Add the onion, garlic, and carrot and cook for 5 minutes.

- Add the remaining ingredients expect for the pasta and the cheese. Set the pressure adjust mode to 50. Set the cook time to 20 minutes.

- Serve over pasta with Parmigiano-Reggiano cheese.

CHAPTER TEN
PRESSURE COOKER STUFFED GREEN PEPPER CASSEROLE

This (Instant Pot) Pressure Cooker Stuffed Green Pepper Casserole comes with all the flavors of stuffed green peppers in an easy-to-make casserole. If you like stuffed green peppers, you're absolutely going to love this Insta Pot casserole.

Ingredients:

- 1 lb. lean ground beef
- 1/2 cup chopped onion
- 2 cloves garlic, minced
- 2 large green peppers, chopped
- handful of spinach leaves, coarsely chopped
- 1 (14.5 oz) can diced tomatoes with juices
- 1 (8 oz) can tomato sauce
- 1/2 cup beef broth
- 1/2 cup long grain rice (uncooked)
- 1 tablespoon Worcestershire sauce
- 1/2 teaspoon salt
- 1/4 teaspoon pepper

- 1 cup shredded mozzarella cheese

How to prepare

- Preheat the pressure cooking pot on the Browning/Sauté setting. Add in the ground beef and onion and cook until the beef is browned and crumbled. Add in garlic and sauté 1 minute more.

- Stir in green peppers, spinach, tomatoes, tomato sauce, beef broth, rice, Worcestershire sauce, salt, and pepper. Lock lid in place, select High Pressure and 4 minutes cook time. When timer beeps, do a natural release for 10 minutes, then release any remaining pressure with a quick pressure release.

- Turn off pressure cooker and pour casserole into an oven-safe baking dish. Sprinkle the cheese on top of casserole and broil until the cheese is melted and starting to brown.

CHAPTER ELEVEN
PRESSURE COOKER GREEN CHILE PORK CARNITAS

Moist, flavor-packed, and fall apart in your mouth tender, these Pressure Cooker Green Chile Pork Carnitas are the ideal solution for a quick family friendly dinner!

Ingredients:

- 2-3 lbs pork shoulder, cut into 6-8 pieces
- 2 tablespoons olive oil
- 1 teaspoon salt
- 1/2 teaspoon black pepper
- 1 large jalapeño, seeded and stem removed
- 1 green bell pepper, seeded and stem removed
- 1 poblano pepper, seeded and stem removed
- 1 lb tomatillos, husks removed and quartered
- 3 cloves garlic, peeled
- 1 onion, quartered
- 1 teaspoon cumin
- 1 teaspoon oregano

- 2 cups chicken broth
- 2 bay leaves

Toppings

- Tortillas (I prefer a flour/corn hybrid)
- Queso Fresco
- Red onion, diced
- Cilantro, roughly chopped

How to prepare

- Rub pork shoulder pieces with salt and pepper then place in pressure cooker and brown in olive oil for 2-3 minutes.
- Add in jalapeño, green pepper, poblano, quartered tomatillos, garlic, onion, cumin, oregano, chicken broth, and bay leaves.
- Give a swift stir and lock lid, then set it to high pressure for 55 minutes.
- Do a natural release and then release remaining pressure with a fast release after 10 minutes.
- Take out the meat from pressure cooker and add broth with peppers to blender and puree.
- Shred meat with fork and then add it back to pressure cooker along with green chile sauce.

- Stir to mix and then serve in tortillas topped with crumbled queso fresco, red onion, and cilantro.

CHAPTER TWELVE
PRESSURE COOKER CRUSTLESS TOMATO SPINACH QUICHE

The quiche is also filled up with diced vine ripened tomatoes and green onions, then topped up with thinly sliced tomatoes and Parmesan cheese. It's a simple to make meal that made plenty for dinner, and breakfast the next day

Ingredients:

- 12 large eggs
- 1/2 cup milk
- 1/2 teaspoon salt
- 1/4 teaspoon fresh ground black pepper
- 3 cups fresh baby spinach, roughly chopped
- 1 cup diced seeded tomato
- 3 large green onions, sliced
- 4 tomato slices for topping the quiche
- 1/4 cup shredded Parmesan cheese

How to prepare

- Put in a trivet in the bottom of the pressure cooker pot and add 1 1/2 cups water.

- In a big bowl whisk together the eggs, milk, salt and pepper. Add in spinach, tomato, and green onions to a 1 1/2 quart baking dish and mix well. Pour egg mixture over the veggies and stir to combine. Carefully place sliced tomatoes on top and sprinkle with Parmesan cheese.

- Use a sling to position the dish on the trivet in the pressure cooking pot. Lock lid in place. Select High Pressure and 20 minutes cook time. When timer beeps, turn off, wait 10 minutes, then use a quick pressure release.

- Gently open the lid, lift out the dish and if you want, broil until lightly browned.

CHAPTER THIRTEEN
CHOCOLATE POT DE CREME

This Pressure Cooker Chocolate Pots de Crème is quick and easy to make. They're rich, creamy and decadently delicious.

Ingredients:

- 1 1/2 cups heavy cream
- 1/2 cup whole milk
- 5 large egg yolks
- 1/4 cup sugar
- pinch of salt
- 8 ounces bittersweet chocolate, melted
- whipped cream and grated chocolate for decoration, optional

How to prepare

- In a small saucepan, bring the cream and milk to a simmer.
- In a large mixing bowl, whisk simultaneously egg yolks, sugar, and salt. Slowly whisk in the hot cream and milk. Whisk in chocolate until evenly combined Pour into 6 custard cups. (I used 1/2 pint mason jars.)

- Add in 1 1/2 cups of water to the pressure cooker and position the trivet in the bottom. Place 3 cups on the trivet and place a second trivet on top of the cups. Stack the remaining three cups on top of the second trivet.

- Lock the lid in place. Select High Pressure and set the timer for 6 minutes. When beep sounds, turn off pressure cooker and use a natural pressure release for 15 minutes and then do a fast pressure release to release any residual pressure. When valve drops carefully remove lid.

- Gently remove the cups to a wire rack to cool uncovered. When cool, refrigerate covered with plastic wrap for at least 4 hours or overnight.

CHAPTER FOURTEEN
PRESSURE COOKER SMOKY HAM HOCK AND PINTO BEAN SOUP

This comforting bowl of Pressure Cooker Smoky Ham Hock and Pinto Bean Soup is loaded with textures and flavors. You'll like the soft and moist ham lending its' smoky flavors to the fulfilling soup.

Ingredients

- Smoked ham hock
- Small onion
- Garlic cloves
- Cumin powder
- Dried oregano
- Ground black pepper
- Bay leaves
- Pinto beans
- Homemade unsalted chicken stock
- Season: Kosher salt to taste
- Garnish: cilantro & minced tomatoes

How to prepare

- You can prepare this delicious dish using 2 different cooking methods for this recipe

- Dump-and-Go Version: This is an easy no fuss method where you put all the ingredients into the pressure cooker, then set-it-and-forget-it. Season, garnish, and then serve!

- More Texture & Flavors Version: Split the beans into 2 sets and place them into the pressure cooker at 2 different times. This version results in an overall flavorful dish full of texture.

CHAPTER FIFTEEN
PRESSURE COOKER KOREAN CHICKEN THIGHS

Delight your taste buds with the umami sweet and spicy flavors in this Pressure Cooker Korean Chicken Thighs recipe. Its fast and simple enough for a weeknight, and classy enough to steal the show at your next dinner party!

Ingredients:

Korean BBQ Sauce

- 1/2 cup gochujang
- 1/4 cup hoisin sauce
- 1/4 cup ketchup
- 1/4 cup mirin
- 1/4 cup soy sauce (I like tamari)
- 1/4 cup sake rice wine
- 1 tablespoon unseasoned rice vinegar
- 1 tablespoon fresh ginger, grated or minced
- 1/2 tablespoon garlic, minced

The Chicken

- 2 tablespoons vegetable oil
- 2 pounds bone-in chicken thighs, skin removed
- 1 medium onion, chopped
- 1 tablespoon ginger, minced or grated
- 1 teaspoon garlic, minced
- 1 cup chicken broth
- 2 teaspoons cornstarch
- 1/4 cup broth or water

How to prepare

Korean BBQ Sauce

- Whisk the ingredients (gochujang through together in a medium bowl. Remove and set aside 1 cup for finishing the sauce.

The Chicken

- Using the pressure cooker or a pan on the stove, brown the chicken pieces on both sides in the vegetable oil. Set it aside.

- Add the onion, ginger, and garlic. Cook until the onion is soft. Add the chicken pieces and onion mixture to the pressure cooker.

- Mix the chicken broth with the Korean BBQ sauce remaining in the prep bowl (after removing 1 cup). Add to the pressure cooker with the chicken.

- Lock the lid, and cook on high pressure for 15 minutes. Release the pressure.

- Take out 1 cup of cooking liquid to a medium sauce pan. Mix the cornstarch with broth or water. Bring the cooking liquid to a boil, and add the cornstarch slurry a bit at a time until thickened as desired. Add in the reserved BBQ sauce. Stir until combined and bubbly.

To Serve

With the use of a slotted spoon, remove chicken pieces to a platter. Pour the sauce over the top, and garnish with slice scallions. Serve with jasmine rice.

CHAPTER SIXTEEN
PRESSURE COOKER VEGETABLE BEEF AND RICE SOUP

This Pressure Cooker Vegetable Beef and Rice Soup is a tasty, hearty meal that comes together fast and is on the table in a flash.

Ingredients:

- 1lb. lean ground beef
- 1 tablespoon oil
- 1 large onion, diced
- 1 rib celery, chopped
- 3 cloves garlic, finely chopped or pressed
- 2 14-ounce cans beef broth
- 1 14-ounce can crushed tomatoes
- 1 12-ounce bottle Original or Spicy Hot V8 juice
- 1/2 cup long grain white rice
- 1 15-ounce can garbanzo beans, drained and rinsed
- 1 large potato, peeled and diced into 1-inch pieces
- 2 carrots, peeled then sliced into thin coins

- 1/2 cup frozen peas, thawed
- salt and pepper

How to prepare

- Preheat the pressure cooking pot using the browning or sauté setting. Add in ground beef to the pressure cooking pot and cook it until browned. Remove to a plate lined with paper towels.

- Add in oil to the pressure cooking pot. Add in onion and celery and cook, stirring intermittently until the onion is soft, about 5 minutes. Add in garlic and cook 1 minute more.

- Add in beef broth, tomatoes, V8 juice, rice, garbanzo beans, potatoes, carrots, and browned ground beef to the pot and stir to mix. Lock lid in place, select High Pressure and 4 minutes cook time. When timer beeps, turn off pressure cooker and do a quick pressure release.

- Stir in peas and season with salt and pepper to taste.

CHAPTER SEVENTEEN
PRESSURE COOKER ORANGE CHICKEN

Pressure cooker orange chicken is one of the easiest and finest pressure cooker chicken recipes to make when you want an Asian meal at home. Soft bite-size pieces of chicken, in a sweet, spicy, orange sauce. This tasty Pressure Cooker Orange Chicken can be on the table in about 20 minutes.

Ingredients:

- 4 large boneless skinless chicken breasts, diced (about 2 lbs.)
- 1/4 cup soy sauce
- 1/4 cup water + 3 tablespoons water, divided
- 2 tablespoons brown sugar
- 1 tablespoon rice wine vinegar
- 1 teaspoon sesame oil
- 1/4 teaspoon chili garlic sauce
- 1/2 cup orange marmalade
- 3 tablespoons cornstarch
- 2 green onions, chopped, optional
- red pepper flakes, optional

How to prepare

- Add in chicken, soy sauce, 1/4 cup water, brown sugar, rice wine vinegar, sesame oil, and chili garlic sauce to the pressure cooking pot and stir to mix. Pressure cook on high pressure for 3 minutes. When timer beeps, turn pressure cooker off and do a quick pressure release. Add in marmalade to the pot and stir to combine.

- In a small bowl, dissolve cornstarch in 3 tablespoons water and add to the pot. Select Sauté and simmer until sauce is thick and syrupy.

- Serve it topped with green onions and red pepper flakes if you want.

Note:

- You can cook rice while you are cooking the chicken. Here's how to do it; Use a 7×3 inch round cake pan or similar dish, and add in rice ingredients. Put a rack on top of the chicken in the pressure cooking pot, and place the cake pan on top of the rack.

CHAPTER EIGHTEEN
PRESSURE COOKER PULLED PORK

Make this irresistible Pressure Cooker Pulled Pork Recipe with your own Dry Rub and BBQ Sauce. Tender, juicy pulled pork exploding with sweet & smoky flavors. Making BBQ Pulled Pork has never been this quick and easy! You have to try it.

Ingredients

- 4 pounds (~1.8 kg) pork shoulder picnic (Cut into 4 – 8 pieces)
- 1 tablespoons (15 ml) olive oil

Pulled Pork Dry Rub:

- 2 tablespoons (25 g) brown sugar
- 2 teaspoons (5 g) chili powder
- 2 teaspoons (4 g) black pepper
- 1 teaspoon (2.4 g) onion powder
- 1 teaspoon (2.8 g) garlic powder
- 1 teaspoon (2.3 g) cinnamon powder
- 1 teaspoon (3 g) kosher salt
- ½ teaspoon (1 g) cumin seed, ground
- ½ teaspoon (1 g) fennel seed, ground

- ¼ teaspoon (0.5 g) cayenne pepper

BBQ Sauce for Pulled Pork:

- 1 medium onion, minced
- 3 garlic cloves, minced
- 1 cup (250 ml) ketchup
- ½ cup (125 ml) water
- ⅛ cup (31ml) maple syrup
- ⅛ cup (31ml) honey
- 2 tablespoons (30 ml) apple cider vinegar
- 2 tablespoons (30 ml) Dijon mustard
- 1 tablespoon (25 g) brown sugar

How to prepare

- Rub the Pulled Pork Dry Rub: Combine all the dry rub ingredients and rub it all over the pork shoulder picnic pieces. Then, put the pork shoulder picnic in the fridge for 30 minutes to overnight.

- Heat up the Pressure Cooker: Heat up your pressure cooker (Instant Pot: press Sauté button). Be sure your pot is as hot as it can be when you place the pork shoulder meat into the pot (For Instant Pot: wait until the indicator says HOT).

- Optional Step - Brown the Pork Shoulder: Add in 1 tablespoon (15 ml) of olive oil into the pot. Make sure you coat the oil over the whole bottom of the pot. Put the pork shoulder pieces into the pot. Brown the pork shoulder on all sides. Remove and set aside.

- Add the BBQ Sauce and Deglaze: Pour in half of the Pulled Pork BBQ Sauce and deglaze the base of the pot. Then, put in the remaining BBQ sauce blend.

- Pressure Cook the Pork Shoulder (See Tips): Place all the pork shoulder pieces into the pot. If you left the skin on make sure the skin side is facing up. Close lid and pressure cook at High Pressure for 60 minutes (see notes). Turn off the heat and fully Natural Release (roughly 15 minutes).

- Fork Tender Check: Open the lid carefully. Take one piece of pork shoulder out and see if you can shred through the meat easily with two forks. If it is not fork-tender, cook for an additional 10 to 20 minutes at High Pressure, fully Natural Release.

- Shred the Pork & De-Fat the Sauce: Use some cool Pulled Pork Shredder Claws or two regular forks to shred the pork shoulder meat. Use a fat separator to separate the fat from the BBQ sauce.

- Season, Reduce, Serve: Reduce the BBQ sauce to your desired thickness. Taste the BBQ sauce and add in additional brown sugar or kosher salt if desired. Place the pulled pork back into the BBQ sauce. Mix well and serve!

CHAPTER NINETEEN
LOADED INSTANT POT MAC AND CHEESE

Prepare this Loaded Instant Pot Mac and Cheese Recipe right now. Piping hot elbow macaroni swimming in creamy cheddar cheese sauce. Sprinkled with buttery toasted golden breadcrumbs, smoky crispy bacon bits, and crunchy scallions. Indulge in this kid-friendly comfort food.

Ingredients

- 16 ounces (454 g) elbow macaroni
- 4 cups (1 L) cold running water
- 4 tablespoons (60 g) unsalted butter
- 14 ounces (397 g) sharp cheddar, freshly grated
- 6 ounces (170 g) mild cheddar or American cheese, freshly grated
- Kosher salt and ground black pepper

Wet Ingredients

- 2 large eggs, beaten
- 12 ounces (355 ml) can evaporated milk
- 1 teaspoon (5 ml) Sriracha sauce or Frank's hot sauce
- 1 teaspoon (2 g) ground mustard

Bacon Bits & Scallion

- 4 – 8 strips bacon
- 2 stalks scallion, finely chopped

Buttery Crispy Breadcrumbs

- ½ cup (31 g) panko breadcrumbs
- 1 tablespoon (15 ml) olive oil
- 1 tablespoon (15 g) unsalted butter
- Kosher salt to taste

How to prepare

- Crispy Bacon Bits: Position bacon on a baking sheet lined with parchment paper. Put it on the middle rack of a preheated 400°F oven. Bake bacon until it is crispy and golden-brown. Set a timer for roughly 18 - 20 minutes. Place them on a paper towel to soak up the excess fat. Cut into bacon bits.

- Pressure Cook the Elbow Macaroni: Add 16 ounces (454 g) of elbow macaroni, 4 cups (1 L) of water, and in a pinch of kosher salt into your pressure cooker. Close the lid and pressure cook at High Pressure for 4 minutes. Do a steady quick release. There is a slight chance that a small amount of foam will come out with the steam. Have a towel around just in case. Open lid cautiously.

- Prepare the Crispy Breadcrumbs: While the macaroni is pressure cooking, heat a skillet over medium heat. Add in 1 tablespoon (15 g) of unsalted butter, 1 tablespoon (15 ml) of olive oil, and ½ cup (31 g) of panko breadcrumbs to the skillet. Toast the breadcrumbs until it is golden brown. Taste and add kosher salt for seasoning.

- Mix Wet Ingredients: In a medium mixing bowl, beat 2 large eggs and mix in 1 tsp (2 g) ground mustard, 1 tsp (5 ml) Sriracha, and 12 ounces (355 ml) evaporated milk. Mix it well.

- Make the Mac & Cheese: Keep heat on low or medium low (Instant Pot: use the keep warm function). Give it a fast stir and check to see if there is excessive liquid in the pot. Drain if necessary. Place 4 tablespoons (60 g) of unsalted butter into the pressure cooked macaroni. Mix well with a silicone spatula and let the butter melt.

- Pour in the wet ingredients and mix well. Add in the grated cheese ⅓ portion at a time and stir frequently until the cheese fully melts.

- If the mac and cheese is too runny, turn the heat to medium (Instant Pot: Use Sauté Less function - Click cancel, Sauté and Adjust button twice) to reduce it down.

- Taste & Season: Taste and season with kosher salt and ground black pepper. You will most likely need quite a few pinches of kosher salt to brighten the dish.

- Serve: Generously sprinkle crispy breadcrumb, bacon bits, then scallion over a bowl of macaroni & cheese and serve immediately!

CHAPTER TWENTY
NEW YORK INSTANT POT CHEESE CAKE

Make this Easy New York Instant Pot Cheesecake Recipe. Pamper yourself or impress your guests with your choice of Smooth & Creamy or Rich & Dense Pressure Cooker Cheesecake with a crisp crust.

Ingredients

Crust

- 10 (120g) graham crackers, finely ground
- 3 - 4 tablespoons (42g - 56g) unsalted butter, melted
- Pinch of sea salt
- 2 teaspoons - 1½ tablespoon (8.3g - 19g) brown sugar (depends on desired sweetness)
- Optional: ¼ cup (32g) all-purpose flour (for blind-baking crust)

Cheesecake Batter (7 inches x 3 inches)

- 16 ounces (454g) Philadelphia cream cheese, room temperature
- 2 large eggs, room temperature
- ⅔ cup (133g) white sugar

- ½ cup (120g) sour cream, room temperature
- 2 tablespoons (16g) cornstarch
- 2 teaspoons (10ml) vanilla extract
- 2 pinches of sea salt

How to prepare

Critical Tips before You Start

- We recommend using a Hand Mixer to mix the cheesecake batter instead of a Stand Mixer. Stand Mixers are usually more powerful, so you can easily over-mix and introduce too much air into the cheesecake batter. This may result in a puffy soufflé-style cheesecake.

Preparation

- Put 16 ounces (454g) cream cheese, 2 large eggs, ½ cup (120g) sour cream on counter-top to reach room temperature. Then, melt the 3 - 4 tablespoons (42g - 56g) unsalted butter.
- **Tip:** this is grave for your cheesecake's success, so please make sure all the above ingredients are at room temperature before you begin. If not, you may end up with lumpy fluff top cheesecake. So don't skip this step!

PART A: Prepare the crust

- Ground Graham Crackers: Smoothly ground 120g graham crackers in a food processor. Or put the graham crackers in a Ziploc bag and roll them with a rolling pin.

- Mix Crust Mixture: In a small mixing bowl, mix up finely ground graham crackers, a pinch of sea salt, 2 tsp - 1½ tbsp (8.3g - 19g) brown sugar together with a fork.

- Perfectionist's Step - Add Flour (if blind-baking for firmer & crisper crust): mix in ¼ cup (32g) all-purpose flour.

- Add Melted Unsalted Butter: Mix in roughly 3 - 4 tbsp (42g - 56g) unsalted butter till the mixture sticks together.

- Line Pan: Line the side and bottom of cheesecake pan with a parchment paper.

- Form Crust: Pour in the graham cracker crumbs mixture. Carefully press down the crumbs with a ramekin or Mason jar to form an even layer. You can also use a spoon for the edges.

Firm Crust

- Method 1 - Freeze: Place cheesecake pan in freezer while you make the cheesecake batter.

- Method 2 - Blind-Bake (for firmer & crisper crust): Place crust in a 325°F oven for 15 minutes.

PART B: Make dense cheesecake batter

- Mix Sugar Mixture: Mix 2 tbsp (16g) cornstarch, 2 pinches of sea salt, and ⅔ cup (133g) white sugar together in a small mixing bowl.

- Briefly Beat Cream Cheese: In a medium mixing bowl, briefly break up the 454g cream cheese by beating it for 10 seconds with a hand mixer using low speed.

- Mix in Sugar Mixture: Add in half the sugar mixture and beat until just incorporated using low speed (roughly 20 - 30 seconds). Scrape down the sides and hand mixer with a silicone spatula every time a new ingredient is added. Add in the remaining sugar mixture and beat until just incorporated using low speed (roughly 20 - 30 seconds).

- Add Sour Cream & Vanilla Extract: Add ½ cup (120g) sour cream and 2 tsp (10 ml) vanilla extract to the cream cheese mixture. Beat until just incorporated using low speed (20 - 30 seconds).

- Blend in Eggs: Mix in the two eggs using low speed, one at a time. Mix until just incorporated (about 15 – 20 seconds with a hand mixer & less time if you are using a powerful stand mixer). Try not to over-mix on this step. Scrape down the sides and hand mixer with a silicone spatula and fold a few times to make sure everything is fully included.

- Pour Batter in Pan: Pour cream cheese batter in cheesecake pan.

- Remove Air Bubbles for Smooth Surface: Tap cheesecake pan against the counter to let air bubbles rise to the surface. Burst the air bubbles with a toothpick or fork.

- Tap until you are content. Make sure the surface is clear of air bubbles or fork marks.

PART C: Pressure cook cheesecake

- Method 1: Pour 1 cup (250 ml) of cold water in pressure cooker. Position cheesecake pan on top of a steamer rack (so, that it's not touching the water). Close lid and pressure cook at High Pressure for 26 minutes and Full Natural Release. Natural release will take approximately 7 minutes. Open lid slowly. Soak any condensation on surface by lightly tapping it with a soft paper towel.

- Perfectionist's Method 2 - Prevent Surface Dents: Put a steamer rack and pour 1 cup (250ml) of water in pressure cooker. Bring water to a boil (Instant Pot users: Press manual/Pressure Cook and set the time to 28 minutes).

- When the water begins to boil, place cheesecake pan on the steamer rack with a foil sling right away.

***Caution:** Don't wait too long to place the cheesecake in pressure cooker, as it'll affect the cooking time. Place it right away once the water begins to boil. This prevents too much water from evaporating.

Immediately close the lid with Venting Knob at Venting Position. Turn Venting Knob to Sealing Position and let it pressure cook at High Pressure for 28 minutes and Full Natural Release. It should go up to pressure in roughly 1 minute. Natural release will take roughly 7 – 9 minutes. Open the lid gradually. Absorb any condensation on the surface by lightly tapping it with a soft paper towel.

PART D: Cool, chill, serves cheesecake

- Cool Cheesecake: Allow cheesecake to cool to room temperature with the lid open in the pressure cooker. Or place it on a wire rack to cool to room temperature.

- Release Cheesecake from Sidewall to Avoid Cracking: After cooling for 10 – 15 minutes, carefully run a thin paring knife between the sidewall and parchment paper to release the cheesecake from the pan. Pull the slightly wrinkled parchment paper lightly to straighten it out for a smooth side.

- Chill Cheesecake in Fridge: Once the cheesecake has completely cooled, place it in the refrigerator for at least 4 – 8 hours (preferably overnight).

- Serve: Remove cheesecake from the refrigerator. The best way to release the cheesecake from the bottom pan is warm the bottom of the pan to melt the butter. You can use a torch or heating pad for this step. Carefully peel off the parchment paper. Enjoy.

CHAPTER TWENTY ONE
PRESSURE COOKER BEEF STROGANOFF

Ingredients

- 2 pound beef, cut into 1 inch cubes
- 3 tablespoon olive oil
- 0.5 cup flour, for dredging beef
- 1 Medium onion, chopped
- 3 clove garlic, minced
- 3 cup Beef broth
- 2 tablespoon Tomato paste
- 1 tablespoon worchestershire sauce
- 2 cup Mushrooms, sliced
- 0.25 cup flour, for thickening sauce
- 0.5 teaspoon salt
- 0.5 teaspoon pepper
- 1 cup sour cream, for last step

How to prepare

Substituting with potato starch will make recipe Gluten Free.

- Put the inner pot into the Pressure Cooker. Put the oil in the inner pot. Press the Soup/Stew button.

- Cut beef round steak into 1-inch cubes, paint in 1/4 cup flour. In little batches, saute the beef in oil until browned on all sides. Add in the flour to make a roux.

- Sauté onion and garlic. Cook until it is translucent.

- Add in the remaining ingredients and stir.

- Place the lid on the Pressure Cooker and Lock. Switch the Pressure Release Valve to Close. Press the MEAT/CHICKEN button. Press the TIME ADJUSTMENT button and set to 20 minutes. Once the timer reaches 0, the Cooker will automatically switch to KEEP WARM. Press the cancel button.

- Switch the Pressure Release Valve to Open. When the steam is released totally, take away the lid. Stir potato flakes to thicken the sauce. Stir in gently and it will thicken in 2-3 minutes with the heat. If you want it thicker, add in more potato flakes. Stir in the sour cream. Serve over cooked egg noodles.

CHAPTER TWENTY TWO
TABOULI SALAD

Ingredients

- 1 cup bulgur wheat
- 1 cup water
- 0.75 cup minced parsley
- 0.5 cup minced cilantro
- 0.25 cup minced mint leaves
- 1 cup red onion chopped
- 3 plum tomatoes diced
- 0.5 cup Lemon juice
- 2 tablespoon olive oil
- 1 teaspoon salt
- 0.5 teaspoon pepper
- 1 Lemon, juiced
- 1 tablespoon diced scallions
- 0 teaspoon olive oil
- 1 pinch salt and freshly ground pepper to taste1/2

How to prepare

- Position the Inner Pot in the cooker. Press Beans lentil button, 5 minutes.

- Add in the bulgur wheat, water, salt and pepper

- Put the Lid on the cooker, lock Lid and switch the Pressure Valve to Closed.

- Once the timer reaches 0, the cooker will automatically switch to KEEP WARM. Press the CANCEL button. Natural release, when the steam is totally released, takes off the lid.

- Let the bulgur wheat cool.

- Mix the lemon juice and the olive oil together then pour over the bulgur wheat, and mix. Add in the parsley, mint, cilantro, onions, and tomatoes. Fold everything together.

- Transfer to a serving bowl garnish with lemon juice, scallions, and olive oil

CHAPTER TWENTY THREE
SWEET POTATO

Ingredients

- 5 sweet potatoes, peeled, diced large
- 1 cup water
- 1 pinch salt and freshly ground pepper to taste1/2
- 0.5 cup Heavy Cream
- 4 ounce butter
- 0.25 cup Brown Sugar

How to prepare

- Put the Inner Pot inside the cooker. Press Beans lentil button, 5 min
- Add in the sweet potatoes, water, salt and pepper
- Place the Lid on the cooker, lock Lid and switch the Pressure Valve to Closed.
- Once the timer reaches 0, the cooker will automatically switch to KEEP WARM. Press the CANCEL button. When the steam is completely released, remove the lid.
- With a wooden spoon, mash the potatoes until it is smooth; add in the cream, butter, and sugar.

- Ladle a portion out. Serve as side dish with your favorite Entrée.

CHAPTER TWENTY FOUR
THAI PEANUT NOODLE

These Thai Peanut Noodles are made with ingredients you probably already have in your kitchen! They're very easy to prepare, truly delicious, and take 10 minutes to whip up!

Ingredients

- 1 pound egg noodle, fettuccini nest
- 12 ounce Thai peanut sauce
- 2.5 cup water
- 8 ounce chicken, cooked strips
- 3 clove Garlic, sliced
- 1 Onion, sliced
- 1 tablespoon Grape seed oil
- 1 tablespoon scallions, green parts only sliced
- 2 ounce cilantro, chopped
- 0.5 lime, juiced
- 1 Salt and pepper to taste

How to prepare

- Put the Inner Pot in the pressure cooker. Put the Rice button. 6 min

- Add in the oil, sauté the onion and garlic for 1 min

- Now add in the chicken, water, peanut sauce, and stir. Then add in the noodles.

- Place the Lid on the cooker, lock Lid and switch the Pressure Valve to Closed.

- Once the timer reaches 0, the cooker will automatically switch to KEEP WARM. Press the CANCEL button. When the steam is completely released, remove the lid.

- Add in ½ the scallions and cilantro, stir. 7. Portion out each serving garnish with scallions, cilantro, lime juice and crushed peanuts.

CHAPTER TWENTY FIVE
PRESSURE COOKER SPAGHETTI SQUASH

Ingredients

- 1 spaghetti squash cut in half
- 1 cup water
- 2 tablespoon olive oil
- 1 teaspoon salt
- 0.5 teaspoon Freshly ground black pepper

How to prepare

- Position the Inner Pot in the cooker. Press Fish/Vegetable button for 2 minutes. Place the canning rack in the unit and the water.
- Place the spaghetti squash flesh side facing up. Drizzle oil over the flesh, then season with salt and pepper
- Put the Lid on the cooker, lock Lid and switch the Pressure Valve to Closed.
- Once the timer reaches 0, the cooker will automatically switch to KEEP WARM. Press the CANCEL button. Natural release, when the steam is totally released, take off the lid.

- When the squash is cool enough to handle pick them up with a towel. Now with a fork scrape out the flesh of the squash and it will fall stringy just like pasta. 6. Top or toss in your favorite sauce and Enjoy

CHAPTER TWENTY SIX
PICADILLO

Picadillo is one of the great dishes of the Cuban Diaspora: a soft, fragrant stew of ground beef and tomatoes, with raisins added for sweetness and olives for salt

Ingredients

- 1 pound ground beef
- 1 cup diced onions
- 1 cup diced green peppers
- 2 tablespoon garlic minced
- 1 tablespoon Garlic
- 2 tablespoon olive oil
- 0.5 cup olives, sliced, stuffed pimento
- 0.25 cup raisins
- 12 ounce tomato puree
- 0.25 cup Tomato paste
- 1 bay leaf
- 1 teaspoon cumin

POWER PRESSURE COOKER XL COOKBOOK

How to prepare

- Position the Inner Pot in the cooker. Press Soup button, 10 minutes. Put the ground beef in the Inner Pot.

- Cook ground beef most of the way all through. Take out and drain excess fat.

- Begin with olive oil; add in the onions, green peppers and garlic. Sweat for few minutes.

- Add in the remaining ingredients stir. Place the Lid on the cooker, lock Lid and switch the Pressure Valve to Closed.

- Once the timer reaches 0, the cooker will automatically switch to KEEP WARM. Press the CANCEL button. When the steam is completely released, remove the lid.

- Ladle into a bowl over white rice. Serve with a side of fried plantains.

CHAPTER TWENTY SEVEN
PEACH AND CHERRY COMPOTE

This delicious summery dessert comes together in minutes.

Ingredients

- 10 peaches peeled and quartered
- 1 cup Cherries pitted
- 0.5 cup sugar
- 1 teaspoon Vanilla Extract
- 0.25 cup water
- 1 pinch salt

How to prepare

- Put the Inner Pot in the cooker. Pour in the peaches, cherries and the left over ingredients. Mix gently.

- Press Rice button. 6 minutes. Put the Lid on the cooker, lock Lid and switch the Pressure Valve to Closed.

- Once the timer reaches 0, the cooker will automatically switch to KEEP WARM. Press the CANCEL button. Natural release, when the steam is completely released, remove the lid.

- Ladle into a bowl.

- Pour over pound cake top with ice cream

CHAPTER TWENTY EIGHT
MEXICAN STREET CORN

You've had grilled corn on the cob before, but this is one step better. A common Mexican street food, it's absolutely delicious, and if you haven't yet experienced its awesomeness, try it today.

Ingredients

- 6 ears corn
- 1 cup water
- 1 cup sour cream
- 6 ounce cotija cheese
- 2 tablespoon Chili powder
- 3 tablespoon cilantro chopped
- 1 lime

How to prepare

- Place the Inner Pot in the cooker. Pour in the water. Place the Canning rack into the inner pot.
- Add in the corn
- Press Fish/Vegetable button. 2 minutes

- Place the Lid on the cooker, lock Lid and switch the Pressure Valve to Closed.

- Once the timer reaches 0, the cooker will automatically switch to KEEP WARM. Press the CANCEL button. When the steam is completely released, remove the lid.

- Remove from the inner pot. Wrap one end in parchment paper for easy handling

- Over a plate, garnish with chili powder, cheese, cilantro, and squeeze of lime.

CHAPTER TWENTY NINE
INSTANT POT TERIYAKI CHICKEN AND RICE

Make this Easy Pressure Cooker Teriyaki Chicken and Rice Recipe and enjoy it. You'll love the sweet and savory teriyaki sauce soaked by the moist and tender chicken thighs over perfectly cooked Japanese rice. Your family will enjoy this delicious Japanese chicken teriyaki rice bowl!

Ingredients

- Chicken thighs (bone-in with skin)
- Teriyaki Sauce:
- Japanese soy sauce
- Mirin (Japanese rice cooking wine)
- Japanese cooking sake
- Sesame oil
- Sugar
- Rice: Water, Medium grain calrose rice
- Garlic cloves
- Ginger
- Cornstarch + water

Japanese style teriyaki sauce is a thickened sweet soy glaze called Tare Sauce (often used in grilling). It's actually very easy to make at home with a few simple ingredients. Generally, a basic teriyaki sauce is made of Japanese soy sauce, sugar, mirin (Japanese sweet cooking rice wine), and Japanese cooking sake.

*Ginger and garlic add aromatic flavors to the Teriyaki Sauce.

How to prepare

- Marinate the Chicken Thighs with Teriyaki Sauce: Mix together 4 tablespoons (60 ml) of Japanese soy sauce, 4 tablespoons (60 ml) of mirin, 4 tablespoons (60 ml) of sake, ¼ teaspoon (1.25 ml) of sesame oil, and 2 tablespoons (28 g) of sugar to make the teriyaki sauce mixture. Taste the blend to be sure it is balanced. Marinade the chicken thighs with the teriyaki sauce for 20 minutes.

- Vaporize Alcohol Content in Marinade: Put the marinade (without the chicken thighs) into the pressure cooker (Instant Pot: press Sauté button and click the adjust button to go to Sauté More function). Add 4 crushed garlic cloves and 1 very thin slice of ginger into the pressure cooker. Let the teriyaki sauce mixture come to a boil and let it boil for 30 seconds to let the alcohol in sake evaporate.

- Pressure Cook the Teriyaki Chicken and Rice: Add the chicken thighs into the pressure cooker with the skin side up. Position a steamer rack into the pressure cooker and carefully place a bowl with 1 cup of Calrose rice (230 g) onto the rack. Pour 1 cup of water (250 ml) into the bowl of rice. Be sure all the rice soaked with water. Immediately close the lid and cook at a High Pressure for 6 minutes. Turn off the heat and full Natural Release (roughly 10 minutes). Open the lid cautiously.

- (Optional Flavor Enhancing Step) Preheat Oven: While the teriyaki chicken and rice are cooking in the pressure cooker, preheat the oven to 450°F.

- Thicken the Teriyaki Sauce: Fluff the rice and set aside. Set the chicken thighs aside. Take out the ginger slice and garlic cloves. Turn heat to medium (Instant Pot: Press sauté button). Taste the seasoning one more time. Add in more Japanese soy sauce or sugar if want. Mix in the cornstarch with water and mix it into the teriyaki sauce one third at a time until the thickness you want.

- (Optional Flavor Enhancing Step) Apply Teriyaki Sauce and Finish in the Oven: Brush the teriyaki sauce all over the chicken thighs on both sides. Place the chicken thighs on a rack with the baking tray in the oven for 5 – 8 minutes.

- Serve: Serve immediately with rice and other side dishes.

CHAPTER THIRTY
BBQ INSTANT POT RIBS

Make this super simple no fuss 4 ingredients BBQ Instant Pot Ribs in just 40 minutes! Brushed with your favorite sweet and smoky BBQ sauce, these soft baby back ribs are finger licking' good. The ideal weeknight meal, last minute dinners, or cook them for your next BBQ.

Ingredients

- 1 rack baby back ribs
- ¼ cup your favorite BBQ sauce (We used Sweet Baby Ray's Barbecue Sauce)
- Kosher salt
- Ground black pepper
- Optional: a few drops of liquid smoke

How to prepare

- Prepare the Baby Back Ribs: Take out the membrane from the back of the ribs with a paper towel.
- Season the Baby Back Ribs: Season the Baby Back Ribs with rich amount of kosher salt and ground black pepper.
- Pressure Cook the Baby Back Ribs: Place 1 cup (250ml) of cold running tap water (or apple cider vinegar) and a trivet in the pressure cooker. Place the baby back ribs

on top of the trivet. Close lid and pressure cook at High Pressure for 16 – 25 minutes. Adjust the timing according to your desire: 16 minutes (Tender with a bit of chew) to 25 minutes (fall off the bone). Turn off the heat and full Natural Release. Open the lid gently.

- Preheat Oven: While the baby back ribs are cooking in the pressure cooker, preheat the oven to 450F.

- Apply Sauce and Finish in the Oven: Rub your favorite BBQ sauce all over the baby back ribs on all sides including the bones. Put the baby back ribs with the baking tray in the oven for 10 – 15 minutes.

- Serve: Take out the ribs from the oven and serve!

CHAPTER THIRTY ONE
PRESSURE COOKER CHAR SIU (CHINESE BBQ PORK)

No need to take a trip to Chinatown! Prepare your own moist and super soft Instant Pot Char Siu Recipe (Pressure Cooker Char Siu Chinese BBQ Pork). Eat them fresh out of the oven. The bite full of sweet, delicious and savory flavors with slight melty texture will make your taste buds crave for more!

Ingredients

- 1 pound (454 g) pork butt meat, split the longer side in half
- 3 tablespoons (45 ml) honey
- 2 tablespoons (30 ml) light soy sauce (not low sodium soy sauce)
- 1 cup (250 ml) water
- A pinch Kosher salt to season

Marinade

- 1 tablespoon (15 ml) chu hou paste
- 2 cubes Chinese fermented red bean curd
- 3 tablespoons (45 ml) char siu sauce (Chinese BBQ sauce)
- ½ teaspoon (2.5 ml) sesame oil

- 2 tablespoons (30 ml) Shaoxing wine

- 1 teaspoon (2.8 g) garlic powder

- 1 tablespoon (15 ml) light soy sauce

How to prepare

- Marinate the pork: Use a fork to poke plenty holes all over the pork as deep as your fork can go. Marinate the pork for 30 minutes to 2 hours in a Ziploc bag with air squeezed out. Take out the pork and marinade from the bag. Pour 1 cup (250 ml) of water into the Ziploc bag and mix it with the left over marinade sticking onto the bag.

- Pressure cook the pork: Pour the marinade mixture into the pressure cooker then put the marinated pork butt meat in the pressure cooker on a steamer basket.

- Season the marinated pork with a pinch of kosher salt on both sides. Close lid and cook at a high pressure for 18 minutes, then 12 minutes natural release.

- Brush the pork: Mix 2 tablespoons (30 ml) of light soy sauce with honey in a small bowl. This sauce is to give some killer sweet taste and color to the outer layer of the pork butt meat. Brush this honey sauce richly onto the pork butt meat.

- Place pork in oven: Preheat oven to 450°F. Place pork in oven and cook for roughly 4 - 6 minutes per side until the honey sauce on both sides are browned with some black bits.

- Serve: Serve the char siu with rice or noodles and the leftover honey sauce on the side.

CHAPTER THIRTY TWO
PRESSURE COOKER PORK CHOPS IN HK TOMATO SAUCE

Make this simple Instant Pot Pork Chops in HK Tomato Sauce Recipe. Soft and moist pork chops, immersed in delicious umami-packed tomato sauce. Super comfort food that both adults and kids are going to love!

Ingredients

- 4 boneless pork loin chops (1.25 inches thick)

Marinade

- ½ teaspoon (2.3 g) white sugar

- ¼ teaspoon (1.5 g) salt

- ¼ teaspoon (1.25 ml) sesame oil

- 1 tablespoon (15 ml) light soy sauce (not low sodium soy sauce)

- ½ tablespoon (7.5 ml) dark soy sauce

Other Ingredients

- 1 medium onion, sliced

- 4 garlic cloves, minced

- 1 small shallot, diced

- 8 mushrooms, sliced
- 50 ml tomato paste (roughly ⅕ cup)
- 2 tablespoons (30 ml) ketchup
- 1 tablespoon (15 ml) peanut oil
- 1 tablespoon (14 g) white sugar
- 1 teaspoon (5 ml) Worcestershire sauce
- 1 cup (250 ml) of water
- Kosher salt and ground black pepper
- 1 ½ tablespoon (12 g) cornstarch mixed with 2 (30 ml) tablespoons water

How to prepare

- Soften the Pork Chops: With the backend of a weighty knife, pound both sides of the pork chops to soften the meat.

- Marinate the Pork Chops: Marinate the tenderized pork chops for 20 minutes with ½ teaspoon (2.3 g) of sugar, ¼ teaspoon (1.5 g) of salt, ¼ teaspoon (1.25 ml) of sesame oil, 1 tablespoon (15 ml) of light soy sauce, and ½ tablespoon (7.5 ml) of dark soy sauce.

- Prepare the Pressure Cooker: Heat up your pressure cooker (Instant Pot: press Sauté). Make sure your pot is as hot as it can be when you place the pork chops into the pot (Instant Pot: wait until the indicator says HOT). This will stop the pork chops from sticking to the pot.

- Prepare the Other Ingredients: Clean the mushrooms with a damp paper towel and make the rest of the ingredients as listed.

- Sauté the Pork Chops: Add in the peanut oil into the pot. Make sure to coat the oil over the whole bottom of the pot. Add in the marinated pork chops into the pot, then let it brown for roughly 1 – 1 ½ minute on each side (don't need to keep flipping). Do not let it burn. Take out and set aside.

- Brown the Onion, Shallot, Garlic, and Mushrooms: Add in the sliced onions, diced shallot and stir. Add in a pinch of kosher salt and ground black pepper to season if you want. Cook the onions and shallot for about 1 minute until soften. Then, add garlic and stir for 30 seconds until fragrant. Add in the mushrooms and cook for another minute. Taste seasoning and adjust with more kosher salt and ground black pepper if necessary.

- Deglaze: Add in ¼ cup (63 ml) of water and fully deglaze the bottom of the pot with a wooden spoon.

- Create the Tomato Sauce: Add in ¾ cup (188 ml) of water, 2 tablespoon (30 ml) of ketchup, 1 tablespoon (14 g) of sugar, 1 teaspoon (5 ml) of Worcestershire sauce, and 50 ml tomato paste (See Tips). Mix well.

- Pressure Cook the Pork Chops: Place the pork chops back with all the meat juice into the pot. Close lid and pressure cook at High Pressure for 1 minute (Electric and Stovetop Pressure Cookers). Turn off the heat and let it fully Natural Release (roughly 10 minutes). Open the lid carefully.

- Taste & Thicken the Tomato Sauce: Remove the pork chops and set aside. Turn heat to medium (Instant Pot: Press sauté button). Taste the seasoning one more time. Add more salt and pepper if desired. Mix the cornstarch with water and mix it into the tomato sauce one third at a time until desired thickness.

- Serve: Drizzle the tomato sauce over the pork chops and serve immediately with side dishes!

CHAPTER THIRTY THREE
PRESSURE COOKER CHICKEN CONGEE

With 6 simple ingredients and 6 easy steps, make this comforting pressure cooker Chicken Congee in Pressure Cooker. Frugal, healthy & easy one pot meal that is perfect for those busy days.

Ingredients

- ¾ cup (173 g) Jasmine rice (using standard 250 ml cup)
- 6.5 - 7 cups cold water (using standard 250 ml cup)
- 5 – 6 chicken drumsticks
- 1 tablespoon ginger, sliced into strips
- Green onions for garnish
- Salt to taste

How to prepare

- Rinse 173g (3/4 standard cup) of rice in the pot under cold water by carefully scrubbing the rice with your fingertips in a circling motion. Pour out the milky water, and continue to rinse until water is clear. Drain well.

- Add ginger, 5-6 chicken drumsticks and 6.5 - 7 cups of cold water (using standard 250 ml cup) into the pot. Do

- not add salt at this point. (The ratio is 1 cup rice to 9 - 9.75 cups of water)

- Close the lid right away and cook at high pressure for 30 minutes + Natural Release in an Electric Pressure Cooker.

- Open the lid cautiously. The congee will look runny at this point.

- Heat up the pot (Instant Pot: press Sauté button), stir until desired thickness & consistency. Season with salt.

- Use tongs and fork to break up the chicken meat from the bones (they literally fall off the bone) and take out the chicken bones and skin (if desired).

- Remove congee from heat and garnish with green onions.

- Serve immediately.

CHAPTER THIRTY FOUR
PRESSURE COOKER CREAMY ENCHILADA SOUP

Welcome fall with this calming, veggie packed, healthy, and tasty, easy-to-make Pressure Cooker Creamy Enchilada Soup.

Ingredients:

- 4 cups low sodium chicken broth
- 3 medium size boneless, skinless chicken breasts
- 1 (3.5 ounce) can chopped green chilies
- 1 yellow onion, coarsely chopped
- 3 large russet potatoes, peeled and quartered
- 1 red bell pepper, cored, seeded and coarsely chopped
- 8 cups peeled, cubed butternut squash (about 24 ounces)
- 3 cloves garlic
- 2 teaspoons salt
- 2 teaspoons cumin
- 1 (8 ounce) can tomato sauce
- 2 tablespoons taco seasoning (store bought or homemade recipe to follow)

- 2 (15 ounce) cans cannellini beans, rinsed and drained
- Additional toppings: pico de gallo, sour cream, shredded cheese, fresh or canned corn, diced avocado, Cholula hot sauce, whole grain tortilla chips, etc

Homemade Taco Seasoning

- 1 tablespoon chili powder
- 1 teaspoon ground cumin
- 1 teaspoon garlic powder
- 1 teaspoon smoked paprika
- ½ teaspoon oregano
- ½ teaspoon onion powder
- ¼ teaspoon salt
- ¼ teaspoon black pepper
- ¼ teaspoon crushed red pepper flakes

How to prepare

- Whisk together taco seasoning ingredients if you're using homemade version.
- Add in chicken broth, chicken, green chilies, onion, potatoes, pepper, squash, garlic, salt, cumin, tomato sauce and 2 tablespoons of taco seasoning to the pressure cooker pot and lightly stir.

- Secure the lid and turn pressure release knob to a sealed position. Cook at a high pressure for 20 minutes.

- When cooking is finished, use a natural release. You can also use a natural release for 10 minutes and then discharge any remaining pressure.

- Take out chicken and place on a cutting board, cover with foil. Using an immersion blender, blend soup until very smooth (this can also be done in batches with a blender but be careful not to overfill the blender! Place a towel over the lid and gently pulse before turning the speed up to blend). Chop or shred chicken and return it to the pot of soup. Add cannellini beans and stir.

- To serve, ladle soup into a bowl, immediately sprinkle with cheese and top with desired toppings.

CHAPTER FIVE
PRESSURE COOKER HONEY SESAME CHICKEN

Pressure cooker honey sesame chicken is one of our easy pressure cooker chicken recipes, letting you make your favorite Asian carry-out meals at home! Soft bite size chunks of chicken in a sweet, sticky sauce. This is a quick, easy to make meal that the whole family will love.

Ingredients:

- 4 large boneless skinless chicken breasts, diced (about 2 lbs.)
- Salt and pepper
- 1 tablespoon vegetable oil
- 1/2 cup diced onion
- 2 cloves garlic, minced
- 1/2 cup soy sauce
- 1/4 cup ketchup
- 2 teaspoons sesame oil
- 1/2 cup honey
- 1/4 teaspoon red pepper flakes
- 2 tablespoons cornstarch

- 3 tablespoons water
- 2 green onions, chopped
- Sesame seeds, toasted

How to prepare

- Salt and pepper chicken. Preheat pressure cooking pot using the sauté setting. Add oil, onion, garlic, and chicken to the pot and sauté stirring infrequently until onion is threatened, about 3 minutes.

- Add in soy sauce, ketchup, and red pepper flakes to the pressure cooking pot and stir to mixture. Pressure cook on high for 3 minutes. When timer beeps, turn pressure cooker off and do a quick pressure release.

- Add in sesame oil and honey to the pot and stir to mix. In a small bowl, liquefy cornstarch in water and add to the pot. Select Sauté and simmer until sauce thickens. Stir in green onions.

- Serve over rice sprinkled with sesame seeds.

CHAPTER THIRTY SIX
PRESSURE COOKER MEATBALLS IN EASY TOMATO SAUCE

Make these Pressure Cooker Meatballs soaked in easy tomato sauce. Bursting with smoky flavors and juicy textures, it is a perfect thrifty make a head freezer meal for those hectic weeknights.

Ingredients

Meatballs

- 1 pound (454 g) lean ground beef
- 4 strips bacon (roughly 80 grams), minced
- 1 small onion, roughly chopped
- 4 cloves garlic, roughly minced
- 1 extra large egg, beaten
- 1 teaspoon (1.8 g) dried oregano
- 1 teaspoon (2 g) fennel seed, ground
- ½ teaspoon (2.5 ml) Worcestershire sauce
- ½ teaspoon (1.5 g) kosher salt
- ¼ teaspoon (0.5 g) black pepper
- ½ cup (31 g) panko bread crumbs

- ¼ cup (62.5 ml) milk

- 2 - 2.5oz (60 - 70g) cheese (we used 40 grams freshly grated Parmesan cheese & 30 grams Mozzarella cheese)

Served with Quick & Easy Tomato Sauce

- 2 cups (500 ml) unsalted chicken stock

- 1⅓ cup (398 ml) tomato sauce

- ⅔ cup (156 ml) tomato paste

- 1 teaspoon (1.4 g) basil

- 1 teaspoon (1.8 g) dried oregano

How to prepare

- Mix the Meatballs Ingredients: Mix all the meatballs ingredients in a large mixing bowl. Add the dry ingredients first, then the wet ingredients. Mix well with your hands.

- Make the Easy Tomato Sauce: Combine all the tomato sauce ingredients in your Instant Pot or pressure cooker. Mix well until the tomato paste liquefies into the tomato sauce. Close lid and pressure cook at high pressure for 5 minutes, then Quick Release.

- Preheat Oven & Test Seasoning: While the tomato sauce is cooking, preheat oven to 450°F. Test the seasoning by cooking a small portion of the meatballs mixture on a skillet over medium high heat.

- Roll the Meatballs: Gently roll the meatballs mixture with your hands into ball shapes. As shown in the video, we like to serve ours with the size that is slightly bigger than a golf ball. You should be able to create 8 – 12 meatballs with the listed amount of ingredients.

- Browning in the Oven: Place a piece of parchment paper on your baking tray and gently place the meatballs on it. Place the meatballs in the oven for roughly 12 – 16 minutes until the top is browned but not dried out.

- Pressure Cook the Meatballs: By now, the tomato sauce should be done cooking on the first cycle. Remove the meatballs from the oven and fully submerge the meatballs into the tomato sauce in the Instant Pot or pressure cooker. Close lid and pressure cook at high pressure for another 5 minutes, then quick release.

- Serve: Take out the meatballs from the tomato sauce. Confirm if the internal temperature of the meatballs are at least 145°F.

- Optional: Continue to reduce the tomato sauce until desired consistency. Taste the seasoning of the tomato sauce and add in more salt and pepper if desired. If you like, add more cheese on top of the meatballs when it's served.

CHAPTER THIRTY SEVEN
POTATO LEEK SOUP

Simple and easy potato leek soup, creamy without the cream! Enjoy this tasty, hearty soup with potatoes and leeks.

Ingredients

- 3 pound Russet potatoes peeled large, diced
- 2 leeks white parts only, large, diced
- 1 teaspoon thyme
- 1 teaspoon hot sauce
- 6 cup chicken stock
- 0.5 tablespoon salt
- 0.5 tablespoon White Pepper
- 1 tablespoon olive oil
- 4 ounce Heavy Cream
- 0 chives or scallions

How to prepare

- Position the inner pot into the Pressure Cooker. Press the Soup button. 10 min
- Add the oil; sweat the leeks and celery

- Add in the other ingredients apart from the heavy cream and garnish.

- Position the lid on the Pressure Cooker and Lock. Switch the Pressure Release Valve to Close.

- Once the timer reaches 0, the Cooker will automatically switch to KEEP WARM. Press the CANCEL button. Change the Pressure Release Valve to Open. When the steam is released totally, remove the lid.

- Puree the soup with an emersion blender or cautiously in small batcher in a blender.

- Add in the heavy cream while blending add salt and pepper to taste.

- Serve

CHAPTER THIRTY EIGHT
SOUTHERN SAUSAGE GRAVY

Ingredients

- 1 pound Bulk pork sausage
- 0.25 cup all-purpose flour
- 2 cup Milk (2% or whole)
- 1 tablespoon olive oil
- Salt and pepper to taste
- Pre-made hot biscuits

How to prepare

- Position the Inner Pot into the Pressure Cooker. Press the Rice/Risotto button to set to 6 minutes. Add olive oil.
- Brown the meat. Drain excess fat. Cook garlic and onions.
- Add in all ingredients into the Inner Pot.
- Place the Lid on the Pressure Cooker and lock. Change the Pressure Release Valve to Close.
- Once the Timer reaches 0, the Cooker will automatically switch to KEEP WARM. Press the CANCEL button.

Change the Pressure Release Valve to Open. When the steam is totally released, take off the Lid.

- Serve over hot biscuits.

CHAPTER THIRTY NINE
AVOCADO CHICKEN SOUP

This is easy to make, just have all your ingredients diced and chopped before you begin.

Ingredients

- 3 Chicken breasts, diced large
- 6 cup Chicken broth
- 15 ounce Diced tomatoes, drained
- 15 ounce Can of black beans, drained and rinsed
- 1 cup Frozen corn
- 1 Small onion, chopped
- 3 clove garlic, minced
- 0.5 Jalapeno deveined, diced
- 1 teaspoon oregano
- 1 teaspoon cumin
- 0.5 teaspoon Paprika
- Salt and pepper to taste
- 2 tablespoon olive oil
- 2 Limes

- 2 Avocados
- Fresh cilantro, chopped

How to prepare

- Position the Inner Pot in the Cooker. Press the Soup/Stew button to set for 10 minutes.
- Heat the olive oil. Add in the onion and garlic. Cook 2 minutes.
- Add in remaining ingredients except garnish. Stir well.
- Position the Lid on the Cooker. Lock the Lid and switch the Pressure Release Valve to Closed.
- Once the Timer reaches 0, the Cooker will automatically switch to KEEP WARM. Press the CANCEL button. Let the steam naturally release. When the steam is totally released, take off the Lid.
- Garnish with lime juice, diced avocado & cilantro.
- You can also add cooked brown rice, crushed tortilla chips, or grated cheese.

CHAPTER FORTY
SLOPPY JOES

Ingredients

- 2 pound Lean ground beef
- 1 onion, chopped
- 1 cup Green bell pepper, diced
- 8 ounce Can tomato sauce
- 1 tablespoon Brown Sugar
- 2 tablespoon ketchup
- 1 teaspoon Ground mustard
- 1 tablespoon spiced mustard
- 1.5 teaspoon Chili powder
- 1 teaspoon Garlic powder
- 2 tablespoon olive oil

How to prepare

- Place the inner pot into the Pressure Cooker. Press the Rice/Risotto button. Set it to 6 minutes. Add in the Olive Oil and heat.
- Brown the meat drain excess fat and cook garlic and onions

- Add all ingredients into the inner pot.

- Place the lid on the Pressure Cooker and lock. Switch the Pressure Release Valve to Closed.

- Once the timer reaches 0, the Cooker will automatically switch to KEEP WARM. Press the CANCEL button. Switch the Pressure Release Valve to Open. When the steam is released completely, remove the lid.

- Serve

CHAPTER FORTY-ONE
CIOPPINO

Cioppino, a fisherman's fish and shellfish stew from San Francisco, is simple to cook, and delicious with the right ingredients.

Ingredients

- 12 Small hard shell clams, in shell
- 12 Mussels, in shell
- 1.5 pound Raw extra large shrimp, peeled and deveined
- 1.5 pound Fish fillets (halibut, cod, or salmon
- 0.75 cup butter
- 2 Onions, diced
- 3 clove garlic, minced
- 0.5 cup Parsley, minced
- 20 ounce diced tomatoes
- 8 ounce Clam juice
- 1.5 cup White wine
- 2 Bay leaves
- 1 tablespoon Dried basil leaves

- 0.5 teaspoon Dried marjoram leaves
- Salt and pepper to taste

How to prepare

- Place the Inner Pot into the Pressure Cooker. Press the Soup/Stew button. Set for 10 minutes.
- Sweat garlic and onion in the butter.
- Add all ingredients except seafood into the Inner Pot.
- Place the Lid on the Pressure Cooker and lock. Switch the Pressure Release Valve to Closed.
- Once the Timer reaches 0, the Cooker will automatically switch to KEEP WARM . Press the CANCEL button. Switch the Pressure Release Valve to Open. When the steam is released completely, remove the Lid.
- Press the Soup/Stew button to set for 10 minutes (without Lid).
- Add the clams and mussels. Cook for 6-8 minutes.
- Add shrimp and fish. Cook 3-4 minutes until cooked.

CHAPTER FORTY TWO
PUMPKIN SPICE RISOTTO

Pumpkin Spice Risotto with sage is my pick for a simple seasonal fall entree that is loaded with comfort food vibes

Ingredients

- 12 ounce Arborio Rice (Risotto)
- 4 cup chicken stock
- 6 ounce pumpkin puree
- 0.5 onion, diced
- 1 teaspoon thyme, chopped
- 2 clove garlic, minced
- 0.25 teaspoon Nutmeg
- 0.5 teaspoon cinnamon
- 0.25 teaspoon ginger
- 0.25 teaspoon allspice
- 4 ounce Heavy Cream
- 2 ounce olive oil

POWER PRESSURE COOKER XL COOKBOOK

How to prepare

- Position the Inner Pot into the Pressure Cooker.

- Press the SOUP/STEW button to set for 10 minutes.

- Sauté onion and garlic in olive oil.

- Add in rice and stir. Add in the remaining ingredients.

- Secure the Lid on the Cooker. Lock the Lid and switch the Pressure Release Valve to Closed.

- Once the timer reaches 0, the Pressure Cooker will automatically switch to KEEP WARM. Press CANCEL. Switch the Pressure Release Valve to Open. When the steam is totally released, take off the Lid.

- Fold in heavy cream.

CHAPTER FORTY THREE
POMEGRANATE LEG OF LAMB

This savory roasted lamb is drizzled with an unexpected tangy pomegranate pan sauce just before serving. It's an impressive dish that's ideal for winter or spring entertaining.

Ingredients

- 1 leg of lamb, boneless (tied)
- 1 cup pomegranate juice
- 1 cup White wine
- 1 cup chicken stock
- 0.5 cup pomegranate seeds
- 4 mint leaves
- 4 clove Garlic, peeled and minced
- 1 teaspoon black pepper, ground
- 1 teaspoon Sea Salt
- 3 tablespoon olive oil
- 2 Tbsp. flour
- 2 tsp. butter
- Garnish: 6 mint leaves, Chiffonade; ½ cup pomegranate seeds

POWER PRESSURE COOKER XL COOKBOOK

How to prepare

- Rub garlic over lamb. Season it with salt and pepper.

- Put the Inner Pot into the Pressure Cooker. Press the MEAT/CHICKEN button. Press the TIME ADJUSTMENT button to set for 20 minutes.

- Place lamb into Inner Pot. Add in olive oil and brown on all sides.

- Add in pomegranate juice. Pour (1/2 cup) pomegranate seeds and mint leaves over lamb.

- Secure the Lid on the Pressure Cooker. Look the Lid the switch the Pressure Release Valve to Closed.

- Once the timer reaches 0, the Pressure Cooker will automatically switch to KEEP WARM. Press CANCEL. Switch the Pressure Release Valve to Open. When the steam is totally released, take off the Lid.

- To make a sauce with drippings, combine butter and flour to form a paste.

- Add in chicken stock and wine to the Inner Pot. Bring it to a boil. Stir in the flour and butter paste. Cook for 5 minutes.

- Garnish with mint and pomegranate seeds.

CHAPTER FORTY FOUR
LOADED MASHED POTATOES

Ingredients

- 4 pound red potatoes, quartered
- 1.5 cup chicken stock
- 1 teaspoon salt
- 0.5 teaspoon pepper
- 1 cup Heavy Cream
- 8 ounce cheddar cheese shredded
- 6 slice bacon, cooked and diced
- 2 ounce butter
- 1 tablespoon parsley chopped
- 2 tablespoon Scallions

How to prepare

- Put the Inner Pot into the Pressure Cooker.
- Press the SOUP/STEW button to set for 10 minutes.
- Add in the potatoes, stock, salt and pepper to the Inner Pot.

- Secure the Lid on the Cooker. Lock the Lid and switch the Pressure Release Valve to Closed.

- Once the timer reaches 0, the Pressure Cooker will automatically switch to KEEP WARM. Press CANCEL. Switch the Pressure Release Valve to Open. When the steam is totally released, take off the Lid.

- Mash the potatoes and add the cream and butter.

- Then fold in the rest of the ingredients,

- Serve

CHAPTER FORTY FIVE
GLAZED CARROT

Turn carrots into a dinner party-worthy side dish with this recipe. It's amazing what a little butter can do to make vegetables taste like dessert--even for picky eaters!

Ingredients

- 2 tablespoon butter, unsalted
- 16 ounce baby carrots
- 4 ounce molasses
- 2 ounce water
- 1 teaspoon salt
- 0.5 teaspoon pepper
- 2 tablespoon dill, chopped
- 2 ounce butter

How to prepare

- Position the Inner Pot into the Pressure Cooker.
- In the Inner Pot, combine carrots, molasses, salt, pepper, and water.
- Secure the Lid on the Pressure Cooker. Lock the Lid and switch the Pressure Release Valve to Closed.

- Press the FISH/VEGETABLE button to set for 2 minutes.

- Once the timer reaches 0, the Pressure Cooker will automatically switch to Keep it warm. Press CANCEL. Switch the Pressure Release Valve to Open. When the steam is completely released, remove the Lid.

- Strain carrots. Add butter to Inner Pot to melt (it will still be warm). Add carrots and dill. Toss delicately.

- Serve with freshly cracked pepper.

CHAPTER FORTY SIX
PRESSURE COOKER BBQ WINGS

If you haven't decided on your dinner menu for Thanksgiving, add this super easy & quick appetizer BBQ Wings to your menu!

Ingredients:

- 2 pounds (907g) Chicken Wings & Drumettes
- ½ cup (125 ml) your favorite BBQ sauce (We used Sweet Ray Original)

How to prepare

- Pressure Cook the Wings: Put 1 cup of cold running tap water and a trivet into the pressure cooker. Put the wings and drumettes on top of the trivet. Close lid and pressure cook at High Pressure for 5 minutes + Full Natural Release Open the lid cautiously.

- Preheat Oven: While the wings and drumettes are natural releasing, preheat oven to 450F.

- Pat Dry the Wings: Remove wings and drumettes from the pressure cooker. Pat it dry with paper towels.

- Apply Sauce and Finish in the Oven: In a large mixing bowl, toss wings and drumettes with ½ cup (125ml) of your favorite BBQ sauce. Place the wings and drumettes in a single layer on a wire rack in a baking tray. Bake until sauce is glossy and caramelized, for 8–15 minutes.

CHAPTER FORTY SEVEN
MOIST AND TENDER PRESSURE COOKER TURKEY BREAST

Turkey breast cooked in the pressure cooker is super moist and soft with only a 30 minute cook time.

Ingredients:

- 6.5 lb. bone-in, skin-on turkey breast
- Salt and pepper, to taste
- 1 (14 oz.) can turkey or chicken broth
- 1 large onion, quartered
- 1 stock celery, cut in large pieces
- 1 sprig thyme
- 3 tablespoons cornstarch
- 3 tablespoons cold water

How to prepare

- Season turkey breast liberally with salt and pepper.
- Put trivet in the bottom of pressure cooking pot. Add chicken broth, onion, celery and thyme. Add the turkey to the cooking pot breast side up. Lock lid in place, select High Pressure and 30 minutes cooking time.

- When beep sounds, turn off pressure cooker and use a natural pressure release for 10 minutes, then do a quick pressure release to release any remaining pressure. When valve drops gently remove lid. Use an instant read thermometer to check to see if the turkey is done. It should be 165°. If it isn't 165°, lock the lid in place and cook it for a few more minutes.

- When turkey has reached 165°, cautiously remove turkey and put on large plate. Cover up with foil.

- Strain and skim the fat off the broth. Whisk corn starch and cold water together; add to broth in cooking pot. Select Sauté and stir until broth thickens. Add salt and pepper to taste.

- Remove and discard the skin. Slice the turkey and serve immediately.

CHAPTER FORTY EIGHT
PRESSURE COOKER PUMPKIN CRÈME BRÛLÉE

This Pressure Cooker Pumpkin Crème Brûlée is classy, creamy custard with the warm, spicy flavors of fall, topped with a thin layer of crispy, caramelized sugar.

Ingredients:

- 6 egg yolks
- 1/3 cup granulated sugar
- 2 tablespoons firmly packed light brown sugar
- 1/4 cup pumpkin puree
- 1 teaspoon vanilla extract
- 2 cups heavy cream
- 1/2 teaspoon cinnamon
- 1/4 teaspoon pumpkin pie spice
- Pinch of salt
- 6 tablespoons superfine sugar

How to prepare

- Put 1 cup of water to the pressure cooking pot and position the trivet in the bottom.

- In a large mixing bowl with a pouring spout, whisk egg yolks, granulated sugar, brown sugar, pumpkin puree, and vanilla together.

- In a small saucepan, whisk together heavy cream, cinnamon, pumpkin pie spice, and salt. Heat over medium heat until cream just begins to seethe.

- Whisking continually, gradually pour the warmed cream mixture into the egg mixture whisking until well blended.

- Pour mixture into six custard cups, cover up with foil, and put three on the trivet in pressure cooking pot. Add in a second trivet and stack the other three cups.

- Lock the lid in place. Select High Pressure and set the timer for 6 minutes. When beep sounds, turn off pressure cooker and use a natural pressure release for 15 minutes and then do a quick pressure release to release any remaining pressure. When valve drops carefully remove lid.

- Carefully remove the cups to a wire rack to cool uncovered. When cool, refrigerate covered with plastic wrap for at least 2 hours or up to 2 days.

- When ready to serve, sprinkle a tablespoon of sugar uniformly over the top of each custard.

- Working with one at a time, move the flame of the torch 2 inches above the surface of each custard in a rounded motion to dissolve the sugar and form a crispy, caramelized topped.

- Substitute 1/2 teaspoon ground cinnamon plus 1/4 teaspoon ground ginger, 1/4 teaspoon ground nutmeg and 1/8 teaspoon ground cloves for 1 teaspoon pumpkin pie spice.

CHAPTER FORTY NINE
PRESSURE COOKER TURKEY STOCK

Pressure Cooker Turkey Stock prepared in your pressure cooker tastes like stock that's been simmered on the stove for hours. But you don't have to skim the foam off the top, nor watch it closely so it doesn't boil too fast, and it cooks in a fraction of the time.

Ingredients:

- 1 roasted turkey carcass, cut into 6 to 8 piece or 2 hindquarters
- 1 large onion, coarsely chopped
- 2 large carrots, roughly chopped
- 2 celery stalks, roughly chopped
- 3 garlic cloves, smashed
- 1 bay leaf
- 5 sprigs fresh parsley
- 3 sprigs fresh thyme
- 1/2 teaspoon whole peppercorns
- 10 cups water

How to prepare

- Pour all of the ingredients in the pressure cooker pot. Select High Pressure and set timer for 30 minutes. When the timer sounds, turn pressure cooker off and use a Natural Pressure release. When valve drops, gently take off the lid.

- Let the stock cool slightly. Pour stock through fine mesh strainer set over a very large bowl or pot. Discard bones, meat, skin, vegetables and herbs. Cover up bowl and refrigerator. When chilled, skim fat from the surface.

CHAPTER FIFTY
PRESSURE COOKER DATE BROWN RICE PUDDING

Ingredients:

- 1 cup short grain brown rice
- 3 cups dairy-free milk (I used cashew milk)
- ½ cup water
- ½ cup pitted dates, cut in small pieces
- 1/8 teaspoon salt
- 1 stick cinnamon
- 1 cup pumpkin puree
- 1 teaspoon pumpkin spice mix
- ½ cup maple syrup
- 1 teaspoon vanilla extract

How to prepare

- Cover up the rice with boiling water and let sit 10 minutes or up to an hour more. Rinse it.
- Bring the milk and water to a boil in a pressure cooker pot. Add in the soaked rice, dates, cinnamon stick, and

salt. Lock the lid in place and bring to high pressure for 20 minutes. Use a natural pressure release.

- When the pressure has released, stir in the pumpkin puree, maple syrup, and pumpkin spice mix. Cook, stirring constantly for 3 to 5 minutes, to thicken the pudding and cook out the raw pumpkin flavor. Remove from the heat and discard the cinnamon stick. Stir in the vanilla.

- Transfer to a bowl and cover the surface with plastic wrap, so it touches the hot pudding, to prevent a skin from forming, and so the steam from the hot pudding doesn't condense and create water on the surface. Let cool about 30 minutes. The pudding will thicken as it cools.

- Spoon into serving cups. Serve warm, or cold, topped with maple-syrup sweetened coconut cashew whipped cream or fresh whipped cream. Sprinkle with pumpkin spice mix.

CHAPTER FIFTY ONE
PRESSURE COOKER STUFFING

Quickly "baked" in the pressure cooker and then crisped up in the oven before serving. This Pressure Cooker Stuffing recipe is so simple; you'll want to serve it all year round.

Ingredients:

- 1 1/4 cup turkey or chicken broth
- 1/2 cup butter
- 1 cup celery, chopped
- 1 medium onion, chopped
- 1 loaf bread, cubed and toasted*
- 2 teaspoons salt
- 1 teaspoons sage
- 1 teaspoons poultry seasoning
- 1/4 teaspoon pepper

How to prepare

- Simmer butter, broth, celery and onion until soft. Add in spices. Pour over bread. Mix well.
- Stuff into a 6 cup Bundt pan. Cover it with foil and poke a hole in the middle of the tin foil. Prepare a foil sling

for lifting the pan out of the pressure cooker by taking an 18" strip of foil and folding it lengthwise twice.

- Pour in 1 1/2 cups of water into the pressure cooking pot and position the trivet in the bottom. Place the Bundt pan on the centre of the foil strip and lower it into the pressure cooker. Fold the foil strips down so that they do not interfere with closing the lid.

- Lock the lid in place. Choose High Pressure and set the timer for 15 minutes. When beep sounds, turn off pressure cooker and do a fast pressure release to release the pressure. When valve drops carefully lift lid.

- Remove Bundt pan and unmold stuffing on to a foil lined baking tray sprayed with non-stick cooking spray. Put in preheated 350° oven for 5 – 10 minutes to crisp up the stuffing.

- Cube the bread and toast on a rimmed cookie sheet in 350° oven for 20 minutes stirring occasionally. Cool bread before continuing with recipe.

CHAPTER FIFTY TWO
PRESSURE COOKER BUTTERNUT SQUASH BUTTER

Smooth and creamy, this Pressure Cooker Butternut Squash Butter is a pleasant treat for your biscuits, toast and so much more. Fresh ingredients make it naturally tasty, nutritious and appetizing!

Ingredients:

- 6 lbs butternut squash
- 1 cup apple cider
- 1 cup brown sugar, packed
- 2 whole cinnamon sticks
- 1 teaspoon fresh ginger, grated
- 1/8 teaspoon nutmeg, grated
- 1/4 teaspoon ground cloves
- 1 tablespoon apple cider vinegar

How to prepare

- Remove the stem and slice off the top and bottom of each squash. Slice in half and remove seeds and stringy fibers. Cut into chunks.

- Pour one cup of water into the pressure cooker pot. Arrange the cut chunks in a steamer basket and place in the pressure cooking pot. Lock the lid in place. Select high pressure and 5 minutes cook time.

- When the pressure cooker has finished cooking and the timer has reached zero, gently release the steam with a quick pressure release. Use hot pads to lift the squash out of the pressure cooker. Let the squash to cool enough to handle.

- Empty the water from the pressure cooker pot, wipe dry and place it back into the cooker. Use a paring knife to remove the skin from the squash.

- Put the cooked, peeled squash into the pressure cooking pot. Add in one cup apple cider and one cup brown sugar. Use a potato masher to mash the squash and mix. Add the cinnamon sticks, ginger, nutmeg, ground cloves and apple cider vinegar to the mixture.

- Lock the lid in place. Choose high pressure and 3 minute cook time. When the pressure cooker has finished cooking and the timer has counted to zero, gently release the steam with a quick pressure release.

- Remove the cinnamon sticks and discard. Use an immersion blender to puree the mixture until smooth. Put into container(s) and cool to room temperature. Refrigerate until ready to serve.

- 2 pounds of cut up winter squash = 2-½ cups of cooked puree.

www.ingramcontent.com/pod-product-compliance
Lightning Source LLC
Chambersburg PA
CBHW052145110526
44591CB00012B/1868